COME ON, BOYS!

Drive the nails aright, boys,
Hit it on the head.
Strike with all your might, boys,
While the iron's red.
Lessons you must learn, boys,
Study with a will:
They who reach the top, boys,
First must climb the hill.

Standing at the foot, boys,
Gazing at the sky;
How can you get up, boys,
If you never try?
Though you stumble oft, boys,
Never be downcast.
Try, and try again, boys,
You'll succeed at last.

Ever persevere, boys,
Though your task be hard.
Toil and happy cheer, boys,
Bring their own reward.
Never give it up, boys,
Always say you'll try.
Joy will fill your cup, boys,
In the by and by!

Never rush into things, boys.
Hurry not with speed
But one step at a time, boys,
And surely, you'll succeed.

BE THE BEST TEACHER!

Of all the earthly things God gives, there's one above all others:
It is the priceless work and effort of committed, devoted teachers.

As you travel the highways of education's domain, As you traverse classrooms near and far,
As you criss-cross the byways and corridors of schools, Be the best teacher you are.

Whether it be at home or at church, At work, or relaxing in a (decent) bar,
As teachers, you must ever deport yourselves well; Be the best of the teacher you are.

Do not ever be content with mediocrity; Never settle for just being on par!
Do not stay at the bottom, where there's room at the top. Be the best teacher you are.

You may be principal, department boss, or year head, or simply a teacher below the hierarchy radar;
If you are at college, primary or secondary school, Be the best of the teacher you are.

Yes, you cannot be perfect, but you sure can excel! If you can't be the sun, be a star!
For in this profession, you touch and shape the future. Be the very best teachers there are!

**Doctors do it using masks and gloves, Priests do it at mass;
Scientists do it in the lab, But teachers do it with class!**

MESSAGE TO TEACHERS

There's nothing to stop you from teaching with class
Even when it seems that your vision has crashed
There's nothing to stop you from sticking to the task
Even though your dreams appear smashed
There's no law to stop you from wearing a smile
Though perhaps you are crying inside
There is never a reason for losing your grip
On faith and hope, which keep you alive

There's very little to gain by recounting your woes
Into every other teacher's ear
For pity and sympathy won't get you far
Though they may be quite kind and sincere

When you teach till you're tired and instruct to the end
Trying to lead your students aright
Though you feel that your teaching is oft times in vain
I say "Keep teaching!" – a new day will dawn bright
Though you live a model life, of love and of grace
And your example shines like the sun
There will be trials and test, and sometimes some thorns
But keep teaching; blessings will run

Keep on with the job of teaching in style
For it's defeatist to sigh and complain
The best thing to do is to pray and renew
Rest, rejuvenate, and start out again
Remember that, surely, at times things will be bleak
But still, never in despair must you grope
For in spite of it all, teaching, and teachers, are a must
And as long as there's life, there is hope

Be a teacher of stamina; be firm, and be strong
Be committed, no matter what comes
Stand up for your calling, alone or in group
Stand fast, though all hell come down!
Stand up for teaching; it's the right thing to do
Stand up, at home, or abroad
Stand up, as teachers, is what I say to you,
Stand up! Stand up! as one stands for the Lord!!

--- And many thanks to all teachers! ----

"To teach is to learn twice."

"To teach is to touch the future."

"Knowledge has never been known to enter the head via an open mouth."

'MUSINGS AND REFLECTIONS'

This Anthology is but a sample of the poetic creations of the Author, who has been writing and reciting and sharing his work for many years.

It is dedicated with much love to my daughter Midecia Precious, and to lovers of poetry the world over.

The collection of poems herein is fairly comprehensive in the quantum of issues and topics covered, and touches on ideas, philosophies, experiences, ideals, and expectations, inter alia. The compositions collectively express emotions, attitudes, advice and positions. They speak to individuals of all ages and strata, and refer to that made by man as well as gifts of the Creator. Honour, praise, congratulations and beseechings appear aplenty, and reflect the musings and reflections of the poet both as a youngster and as a mature adult.

It is hoped, fervently, that above all, the set of poems in this opus will inspire, animate and comfort those who read and meditate thereon. May you, the readers, also be led to engage in musings and reflections of your own.

Happy reading!

Foreword

By:

His Excellency
Sir S. W. Tapley - Seaton,
G.C.M.G., C.V.O., Q.C., J.P
Governor-General,
St. Kitts and Nevis

I commend Michael S. Blake on this anthology. This acclaimed educator and community activist has shared this publication entitled 'MUSINGS AND REFLECTIONS' with us. As a person who is known for the richness of his language expression whether moderating a programme on radio or television or posing a question from the audience at a lecture, he has brought this same high level of English expression in extolling virtues and values of perseverance, patience, excellence, and honesty, or in highlighting the contributions of retired teachers to our collective well-being.

I am sure that these poems and other writings will serve to inspire his fellow citizens and others to aspire to be better human beings. His reflections on Independence and institutional anniversaries of the ECCB, the OECS and ZIZ all serve to jog our memories as to their significant contributions to our national and regional development.

This publication reinforces our values, records milestones along our national and regional paths and creates a tapestry of the lives and events impacting our past and influencing our future. It is indeed a very good read for all ages!

TRIBUTE TO RETIRED TEACHERS

Of all the lovely things God gives,
There's one above all others:
It is treasured, priceless gift
Of faithful, caring teachers.

Many persons have passed through this noble service;
They but sampled this profession fine.
But it was you, sitting here, who stuck to the task,
Who proudly stood the long test of time.

You see, as true teachers, you did not simply teach
The children of our dear land;
But through your precept and honest example,
You left footprints in the sand.

When parents were unavailable, you as teachers were there.
When classmates won't listen, you lent an ear.
You were ever present, to guide your students so well.
You, dear teachers, wise counsel readily did tell.

And so, on this special occasion, sans hesitation,
We salute you retirees with grand commendation.
We hope and we pray with gratitude and with love,
That your life's work will be crowned with blessings from above!

We award you today, we'll remember you tomorrow,
When you left the profession, there was certainly sorrow.
But, thanks do much to you, and the contribution you made,
Our path to the future is now properly paved.

---THANK YOU, AND MAY GOD BE WITH YOU ALWAYS. ---

IN PRAISE OF TEACHERS

Teachers are terrific; their task a vital one.
They're called upon to parent, teach, nurse, pastor – all in one!
Instruct the rising multitudes in matters right and true;
Impart fine skills; guide and direct; all this do teachers do.

They're kind, compassionate and sweet; perform their role with class.
No wonder their contribution will simply last and last.
They temper punishment with mercy, season their speech with truth;
And they treat their students impartially, be they saint or brute.

The students who are in their charge differ as do east from west;
Demand and exact so very much, it leaves little time for rest.
Their wants and needs do vary, as well as their attention span;
Often they take all that they could, but give the least they can.

Parents, and employers, too, rarely lend much aid.
They complain, threaten, criticize; yet teachers, they remain staid!
Working conditions sometimes compete with Hell's (this no joke!)
And still, in this environment, teachers, their duties they never shirk.

Now today we honour those who have recently retired.
Their work, a labour of love, is so deeply admired.
So as they retire at this time, we wish them all God's speed.
We will demonstrate our gratitude by following their lead.

Yes, we value with pride and gusto, how much they've contributed greatly.
May they all receive their just rewards both now, and in eternity.

ODE TO LADY BLOICE-ROBERTS

(On the occasion of the ceremony to bid her farewell from the education fraternity, 27th July, 2012)

Very vivacious describes her so well, she's usually rather avid and sprightly;
Approachable, too, is her forte, no doubt, and many can vouch for her sociability.
Professional – well, what can I say? Except that that's certainly normally her attitude.
A leader in truth, pretty often, in fact. She fits that category with plenitude.
Energetic? Of course! That's Mrs. Roberts all right! She exudes the spirit of someone much younger!
Combine these into one, and what have we got? A seasoned, accomplished educator!

But then she's such a lady, too, you know. So let's delve into this hidden meaning:
After all, professionalism less fitness, to be sure, is akin to bananas sans peeling!
Benevolent she is, and refined as well. She is a role model of large measure;
Unique in her style, approach and m.o; these make her a singular treasure.
Reliable, too, is this lady's domain; one can depend on her co-operation.
She holds tenaciously her beliefs and principles; cherishes them with deep conviction.

Mrs. Bloice-Roberts' tenure and record are sound; her years of service outstanding;
As teacher, Department Head, Deputy Head, Principal, and E.O, her performance is worth emulating.
She's been an asset real rich, a friend and a co-worker esteemed, a labourer of love in the vineyard.
This educator has given 34 years of her life to help young people redeem, and to see them succeed is her reward!

The above, I propose, is an accurate profile of our ally, our colleague, our sister.
'Twill be difficult, I fear, to replace her in full; such like her are fast getting rarer.
So her departure brings sorrow to those of us who know her; she's been so much of a teacher!
We wish her God's speed and His choicest blessings as she leaves; her contribution we'll always remember!

"No entertainment so cheap, no pleasure as lasting as reading."

TRIBUTE TO OBADIAH

Our world is full of people of every class and kind;
They come in shapes and sizes that are too many to define.
They live in huts and houses, in mansions grand and great;
They speak a diversity of languages; we meet many of them by fate.

Yes, people are interesting: some important; all of worth.
Many are lovable, some eccentric, from the first day of their birth.

A lot of people are "just average", the "ordinary man", they say.
A few are so vile and vicious, they hate much the light of day.
Some live their lives sublimely, others experience years of toil.
Many persons are born wealthy; many more in poverty roil.
Some are handsome, even gorgeous, endowed with figures fine;
While there are others who are not comely, with anatomies not streamlined.

But often, in our history, some individuals, they simply shine.
They rise above their co-evals; Excellence their lives defines.
These persons exhibit behaviours that are definitely good;
They are models in society; they teach others, as they should.

Yes, some men, though yet mere mortals, manifest extra-ordinary traits.
These are men who should be honoured, men who good mentors make.

These men make their contribution in all aspects of being:
Some are pastors, police officers, pilots, scientists, are in farming.
Some men make their inputs in fields of service galore;
They are managers, accountants, politicians, chefs, sportsmen and more.

But then there are those who choose to make teaching their domain,
And in opting for this pathway, their influence does remain

To guide their wards and students along the road that's straight,
Enabling them to continue the work they themselves did initiate.

Well, know of such a person: J.O. Williams is his name.
He has blazed a trail of excellence; he has laid a claim to fame.
His has been a life of teaching and leading our Nation's children
From here at Molyneux Primary, to Basseterre Boys, and then.
In his work he was so outstanding, so versatile, so wise.
He left on all who passed through his hands, impressions like a vice!

He taught and led in academics, sports, music, P.E round.
J. Obadiah Williams instilled discipline, in a manner fair and sound.
He showed, via precept and example, clearly and with fun,
That Education is the vehicle and drives one up and on.

I say J.O. Williams offered to us 45 years of teaching of substance.
And ever did he lead his flock to the realm of true brilliance.
He displayed self-less service, spoke with compassion that was sure.
He did not have to do all this, but he did it to ensure
That students of the schools he taught – in fact of the country as a whole-
Could rise from their state of ignorance and want, to the pinnacles of hope.

Yes, the legacy Obadiah Williams left with us will remain for e'er and aye;
We have no excuse to be errant, for he clearly has shown the way.
And so to the students at Molyneux and Basseterre Boys fraternity,
Let us follow in our Headmaster's footsteps, is my sincerest plea.
Yes, we're proud of his contribution; we sure do owe him much.
We're thankful indeed for the part he played in the progress of all of us.
I say our gratitude also rests in the knowledge that 'Sir' is one of God's very own,
And we know that at the end of earth's history, Heaven will be his eternal home.

Thank you, Mr. Williams, Sir!

BE A GOOD CHRISTIAN

As you travel the highways and byways of life,
As you traverse this earth near and far,
You'll be tempted to yield to the lies of the Devil,
But be the good Christian you are!

At home, at church, at work or at play
As youth, your minds are ajar
To Satan's great lie that some sin is all right,
But be the good Christian you are!

Do not be content to imitate others
Do not settle for just being 'on par';
Never use as excuse the failings of others,
But be the good Christian you are!

A Pastor, musician, a deacon – or more
Driving small or expensive car;
Colporteur, usher, choir member, treasurer,
Be the good Christian you are!

Since you cannot be perfect, be as holy you can.
If you can't shine like the sun, be a star!
For it isn't only by works that you make Heaven or not
Just be the good Christian you are!

OH BRETHREN, DON'T WEEP

Oh, Brethren, don't you weep, don't you mourn.

We shall overcome some day
Oh Brethren, don't weep

From African's shore we came long ago
Merely to satisfy the white man's ego
We shall overcome some day
Oh Brethren don't weep

We toiled long and hard in blazing sunlight
For hundreds of years with no end in sight

Eventually in August 1834
Emancipation at last was placed at our door

But still we were treated with neglect and scorn
Simply because of colour Black we were born

Segregation, Apartheid, Discrimination galore
We Blacks have suffered much, and then much more

But despite all this we are moving ahead
We'll improve ourselves until we drop dead

When we go to Heaven, we going to sing and shout
For Jesus the Christ won't chase Black People out.

BLACK LOVE

Come, black brethren, let's sing it out loud:
We here in this Island, we're black and we're proud.
We have overcome much difficulty
We will overcome more.

Many are the problems we still have to face;
There's still much division all over the place.
Crime and violence for sure have to go.
Peace and progress must flow.

We here in St. Kitts sure have our part to play;
As Kittitians we must ensure that each single day
Is used to strengthen our proud heritage.
It's our duty, not privilege.

So whenever we celebrate Black history month
We have to make sure that all 28 days do count
We must always live together in sweet harmony
Let's practise Black unity

Of course we have to work with everyone else
Regardless of race, colour, creed, class or sex
But we first must come together
As Blacks, truly loving one another.

Mt. Carmel at 50

In the year Anno Domini 1965,
In St. Kitts was born- yes, came alive
A movement that grew out of Baptist fervor,
Led then by a man of vision, faith and power:
William Manassah Connor, of course, was his name.
He begat Antioch, then facilitated other Baptists of Fame.

A part of this process saw action here in the east,
From Cayon to Molyneux, as far as the eye could feast
Ably negotiated by a young man of ambition,
Who coupled his enthusiasm with spiritual passion
Through but a mere mortal, of blood, flesh and bones -
None could equal the energy of one Kelvin Jones

And yes, in time, out of pure love and compassion,
We witnessed with expectancy the promising introduction
Of a congregation burrowed deep in Baptist's bowel
Dubbed, appropriately, I submit, this here, Mt. Carmel
Yes, Mt. Carmel arrived, what a glorious day!
Mt. Carmel came, and it sure came to stay!

50 years have come, and 50 years have gone.
And, should Christ tarry, 50 more years will run.
Over this period, Mt. Carmel has seen much success;
With Pastor Jones at the helm, there has been a lot of progress.
Many souls have been won; many challenges trounced;
Untold baby dedications, baptisms and marriages announced.

Today, in June 2015, we celebrate with ecstasy
This enviable achievement of Mt. Carmel's legacy.
Its pastor, leadership and congregants have much cause to revel
In the high-flying feats for which you are known, and excel.
I say heartiest congratulations to Mt. Carmel and Dr. Jones, your pastor
May in God's blessings and protection you continue to prosper.

I say continue with grace this earth journey to run,
So that at its end, you will rejoice to hear God say of you, "My children, well done!"

"A person may make mistakes, but he is not a failure until he starts blaming something or someone else." Ann Landers

"Education must have an end in view, for it is not an end in itself."

Sybil Marshall

CHRISTMAS

Sweet Christmas time is here once more, a season to rejoice
Remembering the Greatest Gift of God's precious choice

C	is for the Christ Himself, born on this glad day
H	is for Happiness which He did bring our way
R	says to Remember the significance of this time
I	Inspires us to show gratitude by living lives sublime
S	is for Salvation, the Saviour brought at birth
T	for The Wise Men, whose gifts brought Mary mirth
M	is for the Manger, where our blessed Lord was born
A	is for All the skeptics who deride Christmas with scorn
S	stands for the Sanctity and Sweetness of Christmas true

This is what Christmas means to me; what does it mean to you?

I'm sure glad that there's a Christmas time when I can pause and say:
"Thank you, dear Lord, for your only Son you sent on Christmas Day!"

CHRISTMAS TIME

Sweet Christmas is here again
And oh, it's so much fun!
For once, all troubles of the year
Are buried, forgotten, done!

Yes, it's Christmas yet once more
The season to rejoice
Remembering the Greatest Gift :
God's most precious choice

The Christ Himself, our Lord Jesus
Was born this great, glad day
And oh, What untold happiness
He sure did bring our way!

Salvation, freedom from sin's grip
The Saviour brought at birth
And like the gifts of The Wise Men
We receive it with much mirth

I love the season; 'tis fresh and fine
A chance to help, to love, to share
The period of gathering
Of all those for whom we care

Yes, teachers, classmates, everyone
Christmas is real and true
For me, it stands for all that's good.
What does it mean to you?

CHRISTMAS TIME IS HERE AGAIN

Well, Christmas is here again; And isn't it a welcome one?
A time to share, to give, to get, to enjoy and have much fun
We love to welcome visitors, friends and family galore
We tell stories, relive the past, share experiences, and more.
The house is cleaned, decorated too, with flashing lights to boot;
The children are all dressed up as well, and don't they look real cute!!

Christmas is when we drink so much – sorrel, of course, a must
Sweet, tasty cakes full of fruits, with turkey roasted to a crust
Many of us buy new furniture, new clothes, new cars , too, you know
Especially now that V.A.T days are here to offer prices that are so enticingly low.

At this special season of the year, there is much revelry as well.
Music, dancing, parades and shows, daily and nightly, swell.
Costumes a-plenty, glitz and pageantry dazzle and entice
And, really, if we're honest, we we'll admit they often please our sight

But, hey, let's stop, even pause a while, and consider this one question:
Isn't Christmas supposed to be a time of meditation
On the advent of Jesus the Christ, the Holy Messiah, Great and sinless One
The Son of God, our Saviour Lord, who offers us all salvation?

Doesn't Christmas mean a time to pray, to thank God for all his mercies?
A time to solemnly recall, the occasion to give him praises?
Christmas is an event, I say, to give thanks to God for His blessings –
Not an opportunity for bacchanal, frivolity, and sinning!

Christians, all faiths included, should never be a part of the frolicking!
Christians of whatever church, must stop in carnival participating.

The way the world celebrates Christmas is totally ungodly,
And followers of Jesus the Christ must stop following sinners so blindly.
I am certain that almighty God does not smile at this behavior,
And is patiently waiting for us to properly honour his Son, our Saviour

So as I wish you all right here and now a truly 'Happy Christmas',
I beg you, Christians, starting right now, to boycott the foolish, worldly, sinful stuff.

Merry Christmas, Everybody!

A little boy asked his father, "Dad, how much does it cost to get married?" The father replied: "I don't know, son. I'm still paying."

WHITHER BOUND?

Whither bound, o sinful man? In which direction travel ye?
Just where is thy soul heading to spend eternity?

Will it be Hell, that place or grief, where one screams and wails and cries?
That site of blinding darkness, where the worm, it never dies?

Or will it be Heaven, Paradise of Bliss, the Home where all are glad,
Sanctified, holy, free from fear, and No one is ever sad?
A home where all is bright and clear, where there is only day;
Where not one ever will grow old, and life is grand always?

Whither bound? Again I ask. As you traverse this earth so round,
How fares your life before our God? My friend, o whither bound?

'Tis easy, without effort, to land yourself in Hell,
But righteousness you'll surely need for to in Heaven dwell.
The pains we have to go through now do make life hard and slow,
But they'll fade to insignificance when compared to Heaven's glow.

Which would you prefer, where will you choose? The choice is yours to make:
A place of abundant, refreshing hope, or an unbearably – burning lake!
O sinner, whither bound?

THE CHURCH

The Church, throughout the ages, boasts an interesting history.
It has done great acts of fortitude, and also many of infamy.
It purports, of course, to be on this earth the representative of God;
It claims, we know, time and again, to be guided by His word.

But, the truth be told, this institution, this 'venerable entity'
Has courted oft much criticism; many question its sincerity.
Its leaders, who shepherds must be, directing their many flocks aright,
Too often, we cannot but admit, engage in actions that stain and blight.

How is it, for example, we ask, that Church leaders oft denounce 'sin',
But they themselves, often blatantly, relish transgressions with a grin?!
Why is it, also, is questioned, with honest legitimacy,
The Church rails against greed and vice, but smiles on sexual infidelity?

Why does the Church now tolerate people entering its 'sacred' halls
Dressed in clothing exposing more than it hides, attire that appalls?
The Church offers to all sundry, games of chance, and 'music' that is so wild,
It's pretty hard distinguishing what's 'Churchy' from what's defiled.

Attending Church these days, it seems, largely seeks to satisfy
An expectancy of society that with this tradition one ought to RITUALLY comply.
So many go to Church apparently, without fail, on Sabbath or on Sunday
And pray to God to give them strength to do sinful things on Monday!

In order to receive finance, and not offend those who are giving,
The Church refuses to censure or chastise those who immoral lives are living.
The Church does precious little to restore those who have sadly gone astray,

And young people, in particular, are NOT nurtured or modelled the right way.

For years on end, decades, centuries, nay – millennia galore,
The Church has been seen to accommodate, to sanction wrong, and more.
It is silent on oppression, injustice, corruption, environmental damage;
Says/ does nothing of ethnic cleansing; helps nary a victim of carnage.

But the Church on earth IS the Church of God: His chosen servant here!
It ought to proclaim His message, His teachings and principles without fear.
It must preach and practise faithfully instructions He proclaims,
For if the Church keeps doing differently, it will lose relevance, and fail!!

"Politics is the Art of looking for trouble, finding it everywhere, diagnosing it correctly, and applying the wrong remedies."

Groucho Marx

WE LOVE THE A.B.C SUNDAY SCHOOL

The A.B.C Sunday School we have today
Did not arise 'just so'.
It started with a vision
From a man that we all know.

Pastor Connor was his name.
Of course, before he was O. B. E.
In fact, e'en before he was a Doctor,
God called him forth to be.

He started off the Sunday School
With 13 simple souls,
But before he left this earth,
It 752 would hold.

The Sunday School has done much good
For many far and near;
For the boys and girls, and adults too,
It has been a blessing dear.

It has guided us through thick and thin;
It has led us oft to Christ.
And now it celebrates 45
It sure is full of might.

And so we congratulate them there-
The Antioch Baptist Sunday school.
I pray it grows from strength to strength
May they stick to God's true rule.

We love the Sunday School!!!

WHAT SUNDAY SCHOOL MEANS TO ME

I do not know just what you think
About our Sunday School.
Perhaps you think it is no good,
Maybe you think us fools.

But even if you think it's right;
Though you may love it dearly;
You'll never know just how and what
The Sunday School means to me.

To me it stands for righteousness.
It is a teacher strong and true;
It helps me to meet and make new friends;
It takes me the Bible through.

But most of all, the Sunday School
Encourages me to turn
To my dear Lord, Jesus the Christ;
Very important for my soul!

TRIBUTE TO THE PASTOR

W	is for William, a sincere man of God
I	is for the Intelligence with which he is endowed
L	stands for the Loyalty he gives both Church and State
L	also for the Love he so generously disseminates
I	is for the Intensity with which he serves his Christ
A	is for the Assistance to all he does provide
M	denotes the man himself, Manasseh of Paradise
M	also means the Meekness that William epitomizes
A	is for the Ability with which he supervises
N	means 'Never give up ', words that this man believes in
A	abbreviates Abhorrence, that's how he does regard sin
S	is for the Simplicity with which he enunciates his sermons
S	also stands for Songs of praise that William does love singing
E	represents Example he sets for all his fellowmen
H	is for the Hope he has to one day inhabit Heaven
C	depicts the Concern, the Care, that Pastor Connor exudes
O	obedience to God's Law, which all other laws it precludes
N	is for the Nation that he does dearly cherish
N	for the Numerous sheep which in his flock do flourish
O	is for the Offer from Bro. Connor to both foe and friend:
R	"Receive of God's salvation; it will keep you to the end."

Mothers – A Tribute

Of all the lovely things God gives,
There's one above all others:
It is the precious, priceless gift
Of caring, loving mothers.

A mother is not simply one who bears
A child into this world;
A mother, though, devotes time and more
This special offspring to mould.

A mother expends her resources and skills
To ensure that the children she is rearing
From infancy to adolescence, to adulthood, yes,
Become righteous and truly God-fearing

When father is unavailable, Mother is there
When siblings won't listen, as well,
Mother is ever present, attentive,
And willing good counsel to tell.

Yes, fathers are important; the whole family in fact,
Contribute to social stability
But the finesse and touch mothers only give
Are unique for our social harmony.

So on this Mother's Day, 2016
We salute all our Mothers so true;
We hope and desire that from start until stop,
Rich blessings will fall profusely on you!

A Mother

She's an angel in truth, a wonder in action,
A mother is often like the fairies of fiction:
Accomplishing feats that ordinary humans cannot;
Performing intricate tasks with hardly a blot.

Imagine with me, that is, if you can-
A world without mothers! Mind you, mothers, not women,
For yes, all mothers are women, but not the reverse.
Wouldn't a world, or even a home, without mothers be cursed?

Because mothers are so vital, their role is so strong,
That many a person, without them, won't last long!

Notice what happens when, for example,
Mother is absent for days – well, what trouble!
Notice what happens when Dad irons the clothes.
So often they look like they just got some good blows!
And washing of the linen – can I say more
Than the fact that it ever looks the same as before?
Unless it was touched by some mother's hand,
As though she works miracles with some magic wand.

Who tidies the house? Arranges it setting?
Who ensures that the colours are perfectly matching?
Who does the shopping, and prepares the dishes,
So that the family's health and nutrition aren't mere wishes?

Who listens to the children without needles interruption?
Then acts on their needs and concerns with acceleration?
And very important! When babies' stomachs grumble,
For sweet satisfaction, whose breasts would they suckle?

That is not to say that mother's main role in life
Is to stay in the home, and be a housewife!
Oh no! The fact of the matter, indeed all agree,
Is that a mother's calling is one of multiplicity.
Mothers' position in the workplace is secure;
Their contribution to the economy is priceless – and more!

I put it to you that life is not only possible,
But worth living as well, because mothers are so flexible.

Thus we harbour no doubt, no reluctance one bit,
To ensure that mothers receive their due plaudits,

So rest and relax galore, to mothers, I say.
Enjoy to the max this, yours, Mothers' Day.

"The moment a child is born, the mother is born. She did not exist before. The woman existed, but the mother, never. A mother is something absolutely new." Rajneesh

FATHERS ARE SPECIAL, TOO

How often is it, when people see us,
They ask: "How is your mother doing?"
Or "Your mom, how's she? Hope she's fine!"
But about Dad, why, hardly anything!
It's mother in this, or mother in that,
Mother, now and forever,
But as for the other important parent,
It's as though there's no one called Father!

Well, mothers are sweet, no doubting there.
A mother surely is crucial.
But don't you forget – how can you really?
That Fathers, they, too, are special?
Listen to me aright, and hear me so well;
Remember this important item:
No one could have come, no one was never born
Without a Father's affirmative action!

We agree, as we must, that often, in fact
Fathers are really found wanting.
But the misdeeds of some, the failing of some Dads
Certainly do not make us **All** loathing!
How many of us sitting right here, right now,
Can testify ever so truly,
That all we are; that all we'll be,
Can be attributed only to DADDY?
So apart from the money that fathers provide,
Besides the protection they offer:
Fathers also give much of their talent and time,
And are a source of affection so tender.
In things spiritual, material, or more,
Fathers do contribute fully.
And people like me, who have both father and child,
Invite you to treat us with specialty!

VALENTINE

V - Valentine, the 3rd – Century Christian martyr of ancient Rome,
Now a most popular figure in nigh every home.

A - Attention and affection on those whom we cherish most,
Are conferred profusely. In our lives, they're first!

L - Love: unlimited, unconditional, unrequited, and more
Is lavished with abandon and relish galore.

E - Enduring and endless describe love that is true –
This, Valentine himself, showed clearly to me and you.

N - Nourishment, to body and soul, that is not food-derived,
Is the essential ingredient of love, especially, of course, to those love – deprived.

T - 'Trusting, trustworthy, tested and tried'.
That these define genuine love, cannot be denied.

I - Inviolable as well, true love must be;
Not corrupted and feigned to or by you or me!

N - Nature itself (as seen in creatures both strong and feeble)
Teems with tales and evidence of love, pure and simple.

E - Endless and embracing, thus, must our love be,
As Valentine's example of yore we imitate loyally.

BE MY VALENTINE!

I have just one request, oh Lady so fine:
Will you please, this year 2016, be my Valentine?
Roses, carnations, chocolate, candy so sweet;
You combine them all. You're a darling complete!

Like Valentine of old, you exude compassion and care;
Of all Dames of finesse, you are by far the most fair.
You're exciting, titillating, inviting, and more.
You represent all that is super and superb galore.

A smile that dismisses depression, - that's yours.
Beauty and passion define your facial contours.
Your demeanor conquers and captivates me.
Please, Royal One, I want to your Valentine be!

"Life is the flower for which love is the honey." Victor Hugo

A DEFINITION OF LOVE

On this Blue Planet, Earth, with evils replete,
Exists a virtue exquisite and supremely sweet:
It's easily the most valuable in any treasure trove;
What is this quality? Let me tell you – 'tis love!

It's more action than passion, more shown than told;
It's as fresh as the morning, yet is ever so old.
It's central to all religions: Must be sent from above!
This superlative goodness can be nothing but love.

None is as forgiving, understanding, or more;
None showers on undeserving culprits such compassion galore!
None is ever more tender, and gentler than a dove.
There's nothing as soothing and as special as love.

Yes, there's an emotion that's evoked from deep down within.
It even covers, says the Bible, a multitude of sin!
It enriches those who have it; makes us truly human – by Jove!
It's that which makes the world go around and be the sane - it is love!

So on this Valentine's Day year 2016,
What is the best present for us human beings?
It's a good, full dose of that which we need so very much of –
It's what Kittitians and all mankind so deeply desire: 'tis love!

LOVE

"What is Love?" It's a question real and deep
For Love makes one laugh, and Love can make one weep.
"What is Love?" Give me an answer, I pray,
Because Love is defined in so many ways.

Some say it's a feeling that fills one with joy,
Be that a man, woman, child, girl or boy.
Some say it's an emotion that we all need to live;
Some say Love fain would take, but would rather give.

Many of the problems that this old world does face,
Would disappear real quick, if Love took its right place.
For many of the ills and troubles of late
Exist simple because Love has been replaced by hate

As Christians, we say that Love is something true;
And we genuinely mean it when we say, 'I LOVE YOU'
So this Valentine's Day, 2016 for sure,
Let's do everything less, but let's all LOVE some more!

"Love is Patient and Kind,... does not insist on its own way."

1st Corinthians 13:4,5

THE O.E.C.S AT TWENTY-FIVE

The O.E.C.S has served us well
Since 1981
From the date of its inception
Amidst much expectation

In Diplomacy, Economics,
In Education Reform
The O.E.C.S has been involved
Ever since it was born

We have benefited, one and all
From this regional Body
It's leaders past and present, sure,
Have led, and led ably

Now we celebrate 25 long years
Of O.E.C.S' life
We look back and reminisce with pride
At its record and profile

As an O.E.C.S student and young boy,
With hope I look ahead
To 25 more years of growth
Under O.E.C.S lead

To young and old, I therefore say,
"Let's celebrate with style.
The O.E.C.S has come of age
And its future looks worthwhile."

Let's support real well this Institution,
Let's give it full line and length.
May it serve us well now and forever,
May it grow from strength to strength!

THE E.C.B AT 25

In the year Anno Domini nineteen eighty-three
Was born a bastion of O.E.C.S unity.
To lend strength and stability to our E.C currency
Was and is the raison d'etre of the E.C.C.B

The coming into being of this financial institution
Was the concretized work of real men of vision.
To oversee, manage and secure our money
Was and is the quintessential task of this entity.

And, in truth, over the years, all 25 so far,
The E.C.C.B has so expertly raised the bar
Of fiscal prudence and the strength of our money supply,
That our E.C dollar is now among the region's most high.

Today, all eight members of this solid bulwark
Can justly and proudly the halls of Central Banks walk.
For much and prolonged 'strength, stability and unity'
Was and is the result of 25 years of E.C.C.B.

No other Central Bank in the region can boast
Of the unique successes that we so confidently toast.
For in spite of the vagaries of the international scene,
The E.C currency ranks among the top most supreme.

Serving eight different countries, six independent,
The E.C.C.B has grown from strength to strength.
An enviable exemplar of (sub-) regional unity;
'Twill do the rest of CARICOM well to join rapidly!!

And so, Almighty God we do sincerely thank
For our servant so faithful- The Eastern Caribbean Central Bank.
Congrats to it for 25 years of efficiency;
This was, is, and shall be its proud legacy!

ZIZ CELEBRATES 50 YEARS

ZIZ Radio came in' 61, to our country's peaceful shore.
A facility to provide and access news, et al., it placed right at our door.

Most welcomed it; some were bemused; But be that as it may,
ZIZ was born for real; it came, and came to stay.

50 years have passed since that grand time, when, for all the world to see,
ZIZ offered to Kittivisians a media house created locally.

Since then, much work, much travail and more, have been its lot, no doubt;
But look around, and you will agree, ZIZ has made us proud.

So let us all - that's you and me - , visitors, and tourists, too,
Fully support our Nation's #1 Station, ZIZ: It's the least that we can do.

"Eternal vigilance is the price of liberty." Wendell Phillips

Z I Z AT 50

In the year anno domini nineteen sixty-one,
St. Kitts & Nevis bade welcome to a new radio station.
To educate, entertain and inform the citizenry
Was the quintessential remit of this news entity

The coming into being of this media institution
Was the concretized work of real men in vision.
To ensure that the people of St. Kitts – Nevis, and beyond,
Are readily served by a reliable radio station.

And so ZIZ was born, in simple circumstance,
With a farsighted vision, and a mission advanced:
To disseminate information, and be a source so sure
Of right education and entertainment galore.

And, in truth, over the years, all 50 so far,
ZIZ has vey expertly raised the e bar
Of being a responsible and reliable supply
Of media outputs of a quality most high.

Today, in 2011, 50 years on,
ZIZ remains committed to its original mission
To be a dependable leader in the press fraternity,
Here in St. Kitts- Nevis, the region, and internationally.

Perhaps no other radio station in the sub-region can boast
Of the enviable successes that ZIZ confidently can toast.
For in spite of the challenges and vagaries of the scene,
ZIZ still ranks among the top most supreme.

Many managers, directors, reporters, other workers, too,
Have all made solid their contribution true –
To provide ZIZ with solid stay-ancy,

Being of immense benefit to you and to me.

And so, to Almighty God we do express appreciation
For our servants so faithful: ZIZ Broadcasting Corporation.
Congratulations to it for 50 years of good work, sure.
We're confident ZIZ shall succeed for 50 years more!!

"Freedom suppressed and again regained bites with keener fangs than freedom never endangered."

Cicero

"Freedom implies the right to do right, not the right to do wrong. It is the right to be wrong, not the right to do wrong."

John Diefenbaker

The LABOUR PARTY AT 80
Congratulations!

This world is full of 'parties' of every type and kind;
Their philosophies and ideologies, far too many to outline.
Some can boast of accomplishments that are really grand and great;
Others are not worth much more than which we defecate!
Yes, their histories are interesting: some are noble, some just rot.
It's important that we distinguish those that stand out from those that not.

Lots of these 'parties' are just average, barely ordinary, we say.
A few have been so simply useless, deserve not the light of day.
Some have done deeds of honour, have worked to serve a cause
That promotes the welfare of others; this they do without pause.
I say some parties, they stand head and shoulders above their rivals.
They exist solely to contribute to the less- fortunates' survival.

Yes, at times, in our history, a party, it simply shines.
It succeeds in most areas; excellence its m.o defines
This party's aims and objectives are inarguably good;
It is a beacon in society; it cares for others, as it should.
This party, though far from perfect, performs in a manner extra-ordinary;
It faces all its challenges with an attitude far from cowardly.

The Labour Party of St. Kitts – Nevis is a party of such acclaim.
It was born out of necessity; now lays a sound claim to fame.
Its life has been one of service; service to its countrymen –
Particularly the poor and needy, the weak, the frail, the lumpen.
It has been quite involved and busy in many fields of action:
Trade Unionism, politics, youth, the media, education.

This party has offered and presented to the people to the people of this land,

Programmes and opportunities for them to be able to stand
On their own feet, and progress to a state of satisfaction,
In a manner that contributes to personal and national elevation.
For 80 long years the Labour Party has been visible
In the attempts to ensure that development is sustainable.

So at this time of celebration, on the Party's 80th Anniversary,
Congratulations are surely in order for this fine, durable entity.
Let's commend its leaders past and present, and work with it to ensure
That St. Kitts and Nevis continues its growth and progress to secure

Dad: "Miriam, there were two chocolate cakes in the pantry last night, and now there's only one. How come?"

Miriam: "I don't know. It must have been so dark, I didn't see the other one."

LET'S RENEW OUR ENERGY

From time immemorial, for years without end,
Mankind has, consciously, opted to depend
On fossil fuels – yes, non – renewable supplies –
To provide us with energy to power our lives.

From all directions, - West, North, South and East - ,
In all lands of the Earth, we have relied on the beast
Of petroleum, coal, oil and natural gas,
To fuel the wherewithal for us to survive.

In Europe, the Americas, Asia and Africa,
And stretching down south to Australasia;
In lands hot, and cold, rich and poor – The story's the same:
They – we – all play the popular 'fossil fuels game'.

Yet the folly of this model is so clear to see,
'Cause these fossil fuels possess NO infinity.
And apart from their limitedness, they are expensive, that's true;
And contribute much to harming our environment, too.

Yes, non – renewable energy, ladies and gentlemen, I say,
He has made and is making all humanity pay
In very serious ways for refusing to see
That renewable sources are what we must tap judiciously.

It's high time we, as one people, begin to realize
That it is simply economical, healthy and wise
To pursue and exploit without let-up or fear,
Other sources of energy that are neither polluting, nor dear.

Solar, wind, geothermal, and biofuels, too,
Exist in abundance, are clean, and can do!
Common sense, our purses, our future, our God
Insist and expect us to adopt this model, going forward.

Yes, this new paradigm we're embarking upon,
Will see us instead rely on wind, water and sun.
We're going green now! – 'Tis about time, really.
For green – not black or grey – best serves all humanity.

So, as a young person, I'm delighted to see
That we in the Federation, with our friends the Taiwanese
Have started well on the journey to green, renewable energy.
It WILL be successful and productive, I promise. TRUST ME!

Remember, Marriage is the number one cause of Divorce!

Marriage is a 3 – ring affair: Engagement ring, Wedding ring, and Suffering.

FROM THEN 'TIL NOW

From Africa's shore we were brought long ago,
To satisfy the white man's racist ego.
To these West Indian isles we were forcibly sent;
Cruel ways to enslave us did the white man invent!

We toiled long and hard in blazing sunlight
For hundreds of years, with no end in sight.
Until, finally, in 1834,
Emancipation, at last, was placed at our door.

But still, even now, many treat us with scorn,
Simply because of colour Black we were born.
Segregation, apartheid, discrimination galore.
We Blacks, young and old, have suffered, and more.

Worst yet, in my mind, I have to admit,
Blacks brutally attack other Blacks real quick!
And instead of together upholding our rights,
Too often each other we curse, kill and fight.

This cannot be right in God's holy sight!
Instead, we must strive to live lives upright.
Let's make sure we get to Heaven to sing and to shout
For up there, Jesus Christ won't chase Black people out!

PROFILE - THE BLACK MAN

Attacked, defeated, forsaken; removed from his native land,
The black man was forcefully enslaved: Done by the white man's hand.

Under these colonial masters, under their repressive rule,
He was kept under subjection, coerced into servitude.

Regarded as pugnacious, ignorant and volatile,
He was mercilessly punished for the most trivial of 'crimes'.
And though he used much strength and power to labour in the fields,
The white man thought it wise and good to feed him scanty "meals"

Classified as livestock, scorned, and exploited, too,
His education was not thought of; he never wore a shoe.
Deprived of clothes and medicine; Denied his basic rights,
Separated from his family. Yes, such was the black man's plight.

For two hundred years of slavery he was kept in this inhuman state,
Until, inevitably, he decided it was high time that it terminate.
Such was his thirst for freedom, such the fury of his attack,
That the white had on option: Die sitting, or try fight back.

But determined to retaliate, the black man fought relentlessly.
Soon the whites, weak and outnumbered, bagged for clemency.
The white man was defeated, His former acts deplored.
The black man was victorious, His rights and liberties restored.

And so, out of his pit-hole, The black man rose with glee.
He had regained his freedom, And he exploited this opportunity.
Yes, now he is terrific: In skill, strength and brilliance.
His successes are prolific, And the whites look on askance.

BUILD ME A MONUMENT

Get your things quick! Come down to the Square!
There's something to tell, which you just got to hear.
But wait a minute – this is no tall tale,
Nor a nancy story, nor yet an account that is stale.
It isn't meant to revisit, to unearth, or to deceive.
But it is for those who in justice and valour believe.

Lots of us here know that at that very said place,
Were sold into slavery myriad members of a race
From which most Kittitian descend, and are rightly proud.
And who, like me, make their voices real loud
In making a fervent and legitimate request:
Let's erect a monument to our ancestors' bequest.

From the mid-17th century, 'til 1838,
St. Kitts did witness a most vile form of hate.
Prejudice underlined it; discrimination its prop;
Brutalized millions of negroes – and others – who could not
At first resist with success its gross in humanity.
But, in time of course, this wicked system did atrophy.
For make no bones about it, believe it you must:
Truth crushed to earth shall ever rise from the dust!

This institution of slavery, so very dirty and base,
Leaves with in our breast, pain, and in our mouths, distaste.
In St. Kitts, it served to demean and destroy;
Deliberate tricks in the enslavers' employ.
And this internecine act, so grotesquely unfair,
Ladies and gentlemen, was supported in that right dey square.

It served and it worked, as we all know so well,
As a market to auction our forebears. How cruel!
So it must be said and repeated for all times,
That Paul Mall, before Independence, indelibly reminds

Those of us aware of our history and heritage,
That our attachment and affinity thereto is for aye.

And at this current time in this period of transition,
We celebrate 177 years of Emancipation.
True, the process is as yet incomplete,
But over the decades we have accomplished much feat.

So now, in this year, 2015
Come as opportunity so glorious for you, me, all human beings,
To commemorate the experiences and struggles of our parents of old,
With a monument solid and sightly to behold.
With UNESCO's support, and that of Government, too
All true Kittitians should rally to see this project through.
Let's break the silence of the agony of our past,
By building a monument that will survive and will last.

A monument that teaches, in definitive terms,
Many lessons that our children so badly need to learn.
Let's build us a monument right there on that site!
I say, build me a monument! Let's set things aright!

Build Me A Monument!!!

BECAUSE OF PIGMENTATION!!

The Black man has to struggle
Has always had to fight
From the time of his creation
Which some say was at night!
His colour is a factor
In all facets of life
Yes, this uncontrollable birthmark
Has led to so much strife

Why so much confusion
Because of pigmentation?

The Black man of every country
In every land and clime
At no point in his history
Has he been sublime
Instead, he's been the object
Of dirty ridicule
For years he was kept as chattel
Had neither home nor school

Why all this victimization
Because of pigmentation?

The Black man is a human being
Possessed of skill and worth
Yet, unlike his counterparts
Has had little time for mirth
The big political offices
The ones of force and rule
Were not at all to be his throne
But rather, he their footstool

Why this unfair distribution
Because of pigmentation?

Today, we say, we've progressed much
Achieving much success
Yet everywhere we look around
Black man in so much mess
Even in 'Black' countries, Blacks are yet to rise
And though many be Black
Yet their thoughts are white;
This represents demise

Why so much downpression
Because of pigmentation?

Many countries are lands that stink
Of Neo-Apartheid galore
Each time Blacks call for freedom
They are brutalized some more
The 'great democracies', they, too
Do aid and abet this crime
Their actions, more so than their words,
Just rubbing in more grime

Why tolerate segregation
Because of pigmentation?

It seems to me that peace will come
And prosperity will reign
When blacks look inward to themselves
And prepare to bear the strain
With a sense of independence
With confidence, pride and skill
Blacks can and will reverse the trend
And put themselves atop the hill!

There's no need for division
Because of pigmentation!!

For the one sole God is the Author
Of all earth; He is its Creator.

"Schooling, instead of encouraging the asking of questions, too often discourages it." Madeleine L' Engle

"An optimist stays up until midnight to see the new year in. A pessimist stays up to make sure the old year leaves."

Bill Vaughan

MAN, JUST MAN

Man's life consists of experiences of every type and sort;
Some are high and lofty, others worth less than nought.
At times it's up, sometimes it's down; it see-saws endlessly.
Some lives are short and brutish; others, long and healthy.

There's often need for Man, - and woman-, this mortal, infinite being,
To give vent to his emotions, to express just how he feels:
His joys, his pains, his faults, his strengths, his expectations, his desires,
His beliefs, ideologies and needs. These must be given free fire.

Thus, Man turns to diverse forms and fora to release his inmost tension;
To reduce fear, to share ideas, for warning and education.
Music, art, drama, dance, prose, signs, song and poetry;
These explain Man's experiences, while honing his creativity.

Without these means of expressing self, unless he employs them as a rule,
Man's sentiments of life's journey would convert him to a brute.
For Man is, in essence, a social creature who has to be and share with others
All that he has and is, in order that he grows and prospers.

So be it with partner, family, friend, or the community far and wide,
Man must communicate and live with Man, so that he may abide.
He also ought ever, always, true, to give honour to his God.
Man, after all, was placed on earth to serve others, and his Lord.

MESSAGE TO MAN

Why has man, in all his mortal greatness,
Relegated himself to such filthy worthlessness?
Why is man so powerful, so inventive, so scientific,
So intelligent, so versatile, so extremely terrific?
The answer, I believe, is known, though not exposed:
His omnipotent Creator allowed him to procure such goals.

Yes, this man, his mighty maker; the great, immortal One,
Planned for his human creation, a life brighter than the sun.
He formed him with such delicacy, endowed him with such treats,
That had man obeyed His commandments, all would be divinely sweet.

But, man rebelled; disobeyed; he scoffed; he broke all of God's (good) laws,
And as a consequence of this action, slid into Satan's paws.
And Satan, grim and waiting, caught him with delight,
And fooled him into believing: without God he was filled with might.

Sadly, from time immemorial, man accepted this advice.
He has embarked upon some ventures which caused him much sacrifice.
Now, oppression, war and hunger haunt and plague man everyday;
He is now crying out for relief, but alas, he does it the wrong way.

Still, man's ability and intelligence are causing him much pain,
For he uses them unwisely, and they'll prove to be in vain.
For though man is 'great', though he be 'bright', he will eventually come to nought,
For if he continues to reject his God, he will suffer, as he ought.

But I'll tell you now what man must do if he wants to avoid this fate;
If he genuinely desires the peace that he so badly desiderates:

Return to God, the Creator, now. Confess and Repent of his foul deeds.
Then, and not until, will he find his goal: Pure joy and total peace.
Do that, just that, and then will God, this ever-loving, merciful One,
Restore to man, His wayward child, true peace, and blessed fun!

"Flatter me, and I may not believe you;
Criticize me, and I may not like you;
Ignore me, and I may not forgive you;
Encourage me, and I will not forget you."

William Arthur Ward

MAN

IN THIS YEAR, 2016, NOW, AS BEFORE, AND EVER AFTER,
THE ROLE OF US, MEN, IN THE UNIVERSE IS MORE PO-
WERFUL, SET AND HEAVIER.

BUT SOMETIMES, PERHAPS TOO OFTEN, AS I LISTEN,'
LOOK AND LEARN,
I HEAR AND SEE SO MANY THINGS ABOUT US, THEY
MAKE MY LONE HEART BURN.
IT'S AS THOUGH PEOPLE NOW HAVE SCANT REGARD FOR
EITHER GOD OR MAN,
AND SO, THEY TRY – FUTILELY – TO WITHOUT US DO
WHAT THEY CAN.

PEOPLE OF ALL CLASSES, ALL RACES, SEX AND CREED;
PERSONS WHO ARE SELFLESS, AS WELL AS THOSE WHO
LUST FOR GREED.
YES, YOUNG ONES, AND OLDER FOLKS AS WELL, OF ALL
SOCIAL RANK AND STRATA,
EVERY CHANCE THEY GET THAT COMES TO THEM, WE
MEN THEY LOVE TO SMOTHER!

WOMEN SAY WE MEN, WE'RE LIABILITIES, A SPECIES NOT
WORTHWHILE.
IT'S AS IF MEN CANNOT AND DO NOT DO ANYTHING THAT
IS NOT WRONG OR VILE.

OF COURSE, WE MEN, IF WE ARE HONEST, WE MUST
READILY ADMIT
THAT TOO OFTEN WE BEHAVE AS THOUGH TO LIVE WE
ARE NOT FIT.
MAN DRINKS, SMOKES, CURSES, FIGHTS A LOT, ABUSES
MOTHER EARTH, AND MORE.
SHIRKING HIS RESPONSIBILITIES TO FRIENDS, FAMILY
AND SOCIETY GALORE.

TOO MANY TIMES MAN HURTS AND HARMS THAT AND
THOSE WHOM HE MUST LOVE.
OF A TRUTH, OUR ACTIONS AS MEN OFT INSULT OUR GOD ABOVE.
WE TEND TO ENGAGE IN CERTAIN ACTS WHICH REALLY
POLLUTE THE LAND:
I MEAN, IMAGINE THE ABOMINATION OF MAN GETTING
MARRIED TO MAN!!!

BUT I PUT IT TO YOU THIS MORNING, WITHING ST. KITTS'
WALLS AND OUT –
THAT OF WE MEN'S INDISPENSABILITY, YOU HAD BETTER
HAVE NO DOUBT!
THE FAILINGS OF SOME MEN, AFTER ALL DO NOT MAKE US
ALL REPULSIVE,
BECAUSE THE FACT IS THAT WITHOUT MEN, MANKIND
WOULD SOON CEASE TO LIVE.

FOR MANY, PERHAPS EVEN MOST US, STRIVE TO DO
THAT WHICH IS RIGHT,
GOING BEYOND THE CALL OF DUTY, NEVER USING THE
FORCE OF MIGHT.
IN FACT, IT IS BECAUSE OF MEN WHY OTHER MEN
CANNOT SIMPLY HAVE THEIR WAY.
THE STRENGTH OF MAN'S GOOD DEEDS
TO OTHER MEN'S WICKEDNESS PUT STAY.

YES, WE MEN PROVIDE PROTECTION, AFFECTION, SKILLS;
OUR CONTRIBUTION IS SO VITAL.
WITHOUT MEN, MANY OF EARTH'S CITIZENS WOULD
EASILY LOSE SURVIVAL.

SO LET US ALL TOGETHER AGREE TO KEEP AND SUPPORT
MAN AS THE HEAD,
'CAUSE LIKE IT OR BELIEVE IT, WITHOUT WE MEN, THE
WORLD IS DEAD!

FROM REFLECTION TO REFORMATION

The 4-H movement is born again, in St. Kitts and Nevis today;
It first saw the light a half- century ago, and for long, did lead the way
In teaching persons, especially youth like me, to be self – reliant, productive, true.
Through 4-H of yore, many persons did learn to practise skills of industry new.

Today, in 2011, now, on this day of April 8th,
We come to launch and celebrate the rebirth of 4-H.
This N G O, this C V O, this 4-H Movement fine
Will certainly yet once again make footprints in the sands of time.
For now, more so than ever, be there thorns, stones or come what may,
The 4-H Club has become once more, this time to stick and stay.

The Head, Heart, Hand and Health together do tell the 4-H story.
The members aim to use them all to bring improvement to society.
Using art, craft, games, education, sports, agriculture, morals and more,
The St. Kitts & Nevis 4-H Club will assist young people galore.

I want you, then, yes, all of us, we gathered here today,
To pledge to support the 4-H Club; not just now, but All the way.
I urge you, in fact, to show your love and interest in 4-H at length,
By joining as a new member. Yes, this will give the 4-H strength!!

LONG LIVE THE 4-H MOVEMENT!

ISLAND IN THE SUN

I think of my dear county,
Shining in the sun
With arms of Hospitality
Outstretched to all who come.

I am proud of my small country;
Here, life is rather grand.
For though we are poor, yet we are rich,
And we own and work our land.

Abounding in rain and nature,
With very fertile soil;
We adore our native St. Kitts:
In and for it we'll always toil.

Industries are abundant.
Agriculture is everywhere.
A set of candid leaders
Who of us do take good care.

Progressing steadily upwards
Despite the stones that block our path;
We are strong, proud and industrious, -
And we have peace; we know no wrath.

OUR FLAG

Our Flag is made of colours five: Green, Yellow, Black, Red and White.
They tell that we, as a people, thrive to prosper, succeed, and unite.

The Green tells of our hills and plains, Of leaves and flowers so sweet;
Of fields of waving sugarcane, And lush grass beneath our feet.

The golden Yellow speaks of light For which these lands are known;
The radiant sun which shines so bright On village, field, and town.

The Black informs of our ancestry, Tells from whence we've come;
Reminds that we're Africa's progeny, Our skin tanned by the sun.

The White is there to teach and stress Full Liberty and Hope;
That in neither despair nor darkness We will, must not ever grope.

And now, the bright Red's for the blood we've shed In our struggles to be free;
Much and long we surely bled To achieve true liberty.

Lets us then love our Flag so dear; Respect and honour it day and night.
It is the Flag of all, far and near; Green, Black, Yellow, Red, and White.

Expression of Gratitude

In 1983, almost 33 years ago
St. Kitts-Nevis and Taiwan became friends for sure
We established diplomatic relations which have been true and strong.
Our mutual trust and respect will surely last for long.

Since then, we've been getting much help in cash and in kind.
The Taiwanese have proven to be friends fair and fine
In areas wide and varied, including sports and education.
The Taiwanese have helped much in the development of our nation.

And so now as students, we say 'Thanks a lot to our friend the Ambassador.
These monetary scholarships do help us well to grow
We promise that we'll use them wisely to improve our situation.
So we do extend and please accept, our deepest appreciation'.

"Safety consists not in the absence of danger, but in the presence of God."

THE KITTIWANESE RELATIONSHIP

A long time ago, in 1983, they say;

Before many persons saw the light of day;

St. Kitts and Nevis became Independent and free,

And began a search for friends globally.

Well, in the wisdom of Prime Minister Simmonds, you see,

And continued by Dr. Douglas so sensibly,

The Republic of China on Taiwan, that's true,

Was chosen as one of our close partners new.

Since then, I can say without contradiction or doubt,

These genuine friends have so often helped out.

Be it in Agriculture, Sports, Health, Education;

Taiwan has been to us a reliable companion.

The entire country, the Federation as a whole,

Has been able, with Taiwan, to achieve many a goal.

For adults, for sportsmen, for school children like me,

Taiwan has ever been a real helpful buddy.

With very much appreciation and gratitude, therefore,

We say, "Thank you, Mr. Ambassador, for your assistance galore".

And so, now, I propose at this award presentation,

Let's all rise and give Taiwan a standing ovation!

"Poetry is the eldest sister of all arts, and the parent of most."

Congreve

"All that is not Prose passes for Poetry." Crabbe

"Poetry is truth dwelling in beauty." Gilfillan

INDEPENDENCE

INDEPENDENCE is not just a word, a cliché or a happening
For us it has significance; its full of solid meaning

I is for INDEPENDENCE, it came in 1983

N is for our NATION we all love so dearly

D is for DISCIPLINE, the drive that keeps us sane

E is for the ENERGY we exert our progress to sustain

P is for the PEOPLE – beloved, proud and free

E is for the EXAMPLE St. Kitts sets for all the world to see

N tells us of NATURE – with her children we are endowed

D is for DEVELOPMENT wise planning has bestowed

E is for EDUCATION which, used right, can only help

N speaks of the NECESSITY to put country above self

C is for the CARIBBEAN; our neighborhood, our home

E, again, is for EXCELLENCE, a hallmark rightly our own

Thus, Independence means for all of us freedom, dignity and pride

It involves hard work and sacrifice, but these we will provide

HAPPY INDEPENDENCE!

INDEPENDENCE AT 14

Independence came in '83 to our country's blessed shores;
Freedom at last from Britain's grip it placed right at our doors.
Some were enthused; others, bemused. But be that as it may.
Independence became a fact of life – it came, and came to stay.

Well, fourteen years since that fateful morn have passed into History,
And we have been in full command or Nation's destiny.
So much has occurred; so much more to come, creates a scenario that excites.
Especially from the point of view of our lack of size or might.

Our people, though, in spite of all, have shown fortitude galore:
We've weathered storms natural and not; they've brought our talents to the fore.
Upheavals here, hurricanes there, instances of violence and crime
Have exacted a toll on our dear Land, but, eventually, in time

We set OUT to prove to all the world what Independence means for real.
With diligence, industry and pride, we were happy to reveal
That we for sure can manage our affairs with certitude,
Guided by a purpose clear, and a vision that is not crude.

So now in 1997, another year of Independence spent.
Our leaders, with a sense of mission, steer the ship of state with acumen.
Congrats to those of us who've toiled to make Independence work.
We recommit ourselves to the tasks, and that our duties we'll never shirk!!

INDEPENDENCE AT EIGHTEEN

Independence – is it possible in phenomenal times like these?
When the Internet, Globalisation, Liberalisation, Lectures and Theses
All seem to point – nay, to declare – with unequivocal clarity,
That to survive in this ya world, inter-dependent we must be?

Just how can mini-states, like ours, our Federation small,
In a world dominated by big powers, on the global stage stand tall?
How much a claim to Independence can we, a miniscule nation, boast?
Have 18 years of Independence really put us 'to the roast'?

Well, since 1983, for true, St. Kitts-Nevis has come far.
In fact, in terms of H.D.I, P.C.I and more, we are the exemplar
To many in the Caribbean, and to the wider Third World area.
Our strides and progress do represent a veritable cornucopia.

In housing, roads, utilities, in tourism and education;
In cleanliness, safety, pride of place, we attracted commendation.
Of course, the ingredients and forces for our upward thrust are surely
not adscititious;
Instead, indeed, the elements in this recipe for growth are purely
indigenous.

Our leaders, our people, too; our land and its sheer beauty
Constitute our resources chief; these we exploit with ingenuity.
With justice, fairness and freedom for all, irrespective of persuasion,
We dedicate our lives and work to bring our objectives to fruition.

So that, with God's help, for the past 18 years, ours is a success story,
Our road of Independence has had fine moments of true glory.
And as we enter now our 19th year of political Independence,
Let's forsake division, unite ourselves, and always look to our Creator
for His guidance.

HAPPY INDEPENDECE BIRTHDATE!!!

INDEPENDENCE AT 25

This year 2008, we celebrate with glee
That grand occasion of our 25th Independence Anniversary.
We have come far, for sure, for none of us as students, see –
Was even close to being, way back in '83

Well, we have seen much progress and development;
As a country we have done well.
And our strides in Education in particular,
We really ought to tell.

Everyone knows, without doubt, that Education is the key
That opens all and any door that leads to prosperity.
And so we have to give many thanks for our Education here;
It can hold its own – and excel, too --- any time and everywhere.

But let us always be aware that whatever we achieve,
Be it in Education or not, we must know and believe
That it is God, and only God, whose mercy and whose love
Are responsible for all good things, which are sent from above.

So on this occasion of our Independence,
As we enjoy ourselves galore,
Let us give thanks and praise to God,
So that we can look forward to 25 more.

Happy Independence to all!!!

Urgent Message To Our Youth

Youth, you are the future, thus you are our hope,
And so, in irresponsibility, you must never, ever grope.
You have within your being the wherewithal, it's true.
To lead our growing nation in paths that are bright and new.
Your potential, your ability, are within your breast inherent,
And the competency to do well lies inside you latent

Youth, you are the future; on you we must depend
To ensure that our cherished values never know an end
Our History, our heritage, our culture, our custom,
Our legacy, our aspirations, you cannot ever abandon.
You must be our standard bearers, champions of what is right,
Preservers of our unique traditions; you must set your aims real high.

Youth, you are the future, you represent continuity;
So to you is entrusted the task of perpetuating prosperity.
A sense of fairness and justice must be your guiding light,
Imbued with a spirit of fraternity and co-operation – this excites!
Compassion, tolerance, forgiveness: these values you must practise.
Put an end to insolence, crime and violence. In fact, you ought to cease all malice!

Yes, the robberies and the murders that plague us now so much,
Are committed far, far too often by youth who must be out of touch!
The killings of our young men: our brothers, sons and friends,
Indicate rage, revenge, intolerance.– These simply have to end!
For youth to have a future, you must live, learn, love and care.
You must stop destroying our country – from gangs and guns you must stay clear!

Youth, you are the future. That means so very much!
With positive trends and developments, you simply have to keep in touch,

Read widely; study plenty; discuss and exchange the news,
All the while listening to and respecting the other person's views
Be au fait with what is happening in science and technology,
If you do not keep fully abreast, you will not succeed sufficiently.

Youth, you are future, but with the present you must also contend,
And you must be knowledgeable of your History – a truly useful blend
Of the ingredients that are crucial for youth to have success.
And, of course, if you, as young people, the Creator he must bless,
You must respect your elders: – parents teachers, those in authority.
And then, my dear young people, you'll be set for posterity!
LIVE AND LET LIVE.

A man inserted an 'Ad' in the newspaper: "Wife wanted." The next day, he received a hundred letters, all saying the same thing: "You can have mine!"

The Commonwealth

The Commonwealth of Nations – An association good.
Its members number 54. They're united, as they should

C   stands for Community – That's what the Commonwealth symbolizes.

O   is for the Organization, with fewer failures than successes.

M   is for the members, of which our dear St. Kitts is just one.

M   again, for the Miles of road that the Commonwealth has run

O   once more, this time to tell of Order. This is vital

N   for the Necessity to co-operate for survival

W   is for its Wealth of talent, expertise and wisdom.

E   is for Every person, who is important in this union.

A   is for the Assistance that is regularly given.

L   represents Loyalty to Queen Elizabeth, the Commonwealth's Captain

T   is for togetherness which we must show with clarity.

H   finally, for the Hope we have to live in peace and unity

Yes, teachers, students, it's clear to see that the Commonwealth is beneficial.
We're proud to be a part of it; our support for it will be eternal.

THE COMMONWEALTH

The Commonwealth is a group of lands, Of people far and wide;
Combining climes and customs, too, That span a great divide.

It was begun many years ago, Long before I saw the light of day,
But through rough and smooth, through thick and thin,
It surely has come a long, long way.

From nations mighty in size and strength To the puny ones void of power:
Canada, India, Great Britain, plus Seychelles, Tuvalu, St. Christopher.

Many benefits we have derived From membership of this Union:
In matters of Health, Agriculture, Sports, Diplomacy, Law, Education.

This year, 2012, of course, The Commonwealth's Head - Her Majesty-
Queen Elizabeth 2, Celebrates sixty full years
As Monarch of many a member – country.

This grand occasion, The Diamond Jubilee, Is reason to rejoice and be happy,
Since she is also Queen of St. Kitts and Nevis, and is deserving of respect aplenty.

So I encourage and urge students, teachers, all, To support the Commonwealth ever.

Our participation therein does contribute To making our dear country better!

A HAPPY NEW YEAR!
2016

A 'Happy New Year'- a greeting so old
Yet filled with hope and good wishes untold.
A Happy New Year! - what more can one ask?
It says that may you this year in success do bask.
A Happy New Year! - what more can one give,
Expressing, succinctly, the desire that you live
In peace and prosperity, with good health to boot?
Yes, a Happy New Year! Is my prayer for you.

It's also a new beginning, a fresh era of sorts;
Of regress and peril may you truly have nought.
366 more days of time have begun,
And except the Messiah returns, they surely will run.
May family, neigbours and friends, and people everywhere
Be recipients throughout of blessings so rare.
Let war be no more; replace it with love;
Allow our minds, hearts and soil to be attuned to Above.

A Happy New Year ! – another new opening unfolds!
What grand occasion ! What opportunities to hold !
The past year and years have brought vicissitudes: -
Many instances of vice, few of rectitude.
Advances in medicine, science and technology were good,
But sadly, they outpaced progress in tolerance and brotherhood.
But now we're on the threshold of a brand new leap year;
Let's face it and live it without despair or fear.

My prayer so earnest, my expectation so sound:
That this New Year, starting now, with health and contentment abounds.
Trust always, only in God, does the good Bible say,
And it will, this New Year, as before, great dividends pay.
A Happy New year! – this request I repeat.
May this new year be for you one filled with fine treat.

Yes, rest all your fears and concerns in God, and I put it to you: A HAPPY NEW YEAR will be yours all through!

Teacher: "John, you missed school last Friday!"
John: "Wrong, teacher. I was absent, but I sure didn't miss it!!"

"If you think Education is expensive, try ignorance!"

"Ignorance is a night of the mind, but a night without moon or stars." Mao Tse Tung

YOUR MONEY, YOUR FUTURE

Your money is your future, no doubt about it;
Your money is your future, how true!
Your money is your future; that's quite explicit:
Without money, your future is blue!
So, with your money you must be wise;
Work, earn, and save some for sure.
Take some of your money and economize.
Do that, and your future is secure!

"One merit of poetry few persons will deny: it says more in fewer words than prose." Voltaire

"With me, poetry has not been a purpose, but a passion."

Edgar Allan Poe

Pre- Schoolers' Graduation

How pleased I am - And I am
Sure you are, too,
To celebrate today
This grand event of Graduation,
In this very special way.

Although it happens every year,
For quite a long time now,
We still look forward so eagerly;
It's really glorious, somehow.

Those little ones, our boys and girls,
So innocent, so sweet!
They're very precious in our eyes,
We love them with each heartbeat!

We're proud to see them grow like this,
Here at this outstanding pre-school
For though they're so small, so dependent
They've begun to learn good rules!

And so I'm happy to report
On this lovely Graduation Day,
We're thankful for their caregivers
And teachers, all the way.

As our children now move on and up
To the schools at the level of primary
We're confident and we're satisfied
That they'll continue to do excellently

NEW STANDARDS, NEW OPPORTUNITIES, NEW SUCCESSES.

Education Week is here again – a time for deep reflection;
A time to intro-spect, to strategize, a time for celebration.
All members of this discipline, top echelons and rank-and-file,
Now pause to show to all the world, with pleasure and with style
That Education is about quality, and that it sure espouses
New standards, new opportunities, and, of course, new successes.

Literacy, discipline, rectitude and professional acumen
Are hallmarks of Education's thrust, not once, but over and again.
You see, Education best offers to all, the method and the vehicle
That takes one from ignorance and want to the very topmost pinnacle.
Education Week, then, this year so very proudly establishes
That it promotes wholeheartedly new standards, new opportunities, new successes.

In behavior, attitude, in skills, in performance and achievement,
Persons exposed to education, by and large do boast improvement.
Education, too, provides so well intellectual, mental and moral wherewithal
To enable those who receive it much to reject behaviours that are anti-social.
And so, this year, 2011, let us relish and celebrate without excesses
Education Week, as it embraces new standards, new opportunities, new successes.

HAPPY EDUCATION WEEK TO ALL!!

THE BEST SCHOOL OF ALL
(Basseterre Boys' School!)

It's good to be back at the school we knew, the land of youth and dreams;
To greet again the rule knew before we took the stream.
Though long we've missed the sight of her, our hearts cannot forget.
We have not lost the old delight of her; we keep her honour yet.

To speak of fame, a venture is, there's little here can bide;
But we may face the centuries and dare the deepening tide:
For though the dust that's part of us to dust again be gone,
Here at Basseterre Boys beats the heart of us, this school we've handed on.

The teachers who tanned the hide of us, our daily foes and friends,
They shall not lose their pride of us, however the journey ends.
Their voice, to us who sing of it, ever more its message bears,
And all the world shall ring of it, for all we are be theirs.

Yes, I speak with pride and much acclaim of this Basseterre Boys' School;
How very much I cherished her: her halls, her class, her rules.
Basseterre Boys was the best of all, the grandest school there was
And this is why, you'll understand, why being here is so much missed.

And now in 2015, you see, and with our memories real nigh,
I come to repeat so loud and clear that our love for her will never die.
Congrats! On your years so far of triumph and progress;
I wish you had many more years of superlative success!

HEIL TO OUR SCHOOLS!

All over the island, in villages proud and strong,
Stand learning institutions to one of which all of us belong.
They began their work with/for us during PAM's or LABOUR's rule;
These bastions of education, of course, are our worthy high schools.

Over the years, as time has passed, they have done a job real grand,
Providing students with skills and attitudes that spread throughout the land.
Knowledge, too, they dispense with ease, using teaching as a basic tool,
Making those who passed through their doors real proud of their High School.

In sports, academics, morals, and more, do our various High Schools excel.
Their diverse but related philosophy of education their mottos do truly tell.
And, throughout the years, to their community, and extending beyond, as a pool,
None has contributed to their development, none, like our cherished High Schools.

Yes, these Schools have produced some fine sons of the soil, and daughters, as well;
Who have done to their Schools justice true:
In education, medicine, law, security, business. Sports, engineering, and tourism, too.
These Schools have outputted many a person whose contribution truly outstands:
And together they are responsible for the progress visible in our land.

BUT- What's happening now? It's abundantly clear we're NOT doing the best that we could;

We're not performing with quality, the pride, the ability or effort that we should!
Too many acts of violence and of sass – too many pants half-way down!
Too much insolence, not enough care taken of texts, too many students playing the clown!

There is too much lassitude, lateness, poor parental input, too; many students simply wasting
time
Instead of coming to learn manners, discipline and fine skills, very many go just for to lime!
Let's stop all this crap! Let's settle down now! Let's once again set and practise standards real
High!
Yes, let's make sure one more time that the regions best schools are none but our own Secondary Highs!

"Much have I sorrowed, Learning to my cost, That a book that's borrowed, Is a book that's lost."

Arthur Guiterman

Seize the moment

'Times Hard', some people say. 'Things real rough for true.'
'I can hardly make ends meet', is what they say to me and you.
They make it sound as though things simply could not get worse.
And they give the impression, that this country, it is really, truly cursed

But when I pause and think of some other places I know
It's poverty and misery and want and instability galore
Now I am certainly not saying that we cannot improve
But we are better off than a lot of them; and that is the plain truth.

REFRAIN

I say, things really cannot be that bad,
For although we are far from perfect
There is very much to make us glad.
Many people, many countries, have it far worse than we
So the answer to their whinings, is to seize the moment confidently!

Seize the moment – be wise and smart!
Think with your brain, and not with your heart!
Seize the moment - opportunity is there
To make things better - you just have to prepare

People of St. Kitts, believe me, we are blessed
Many visitors, with us are highly impressed
And inspite of the fact that more could be done,
Many people do well in this land of sea and sun

My solution to this, is simple, you see:
We must seize the moment, with no temerity.
Trust in God we have to; and to help out each other
After all, remember, we are our brother's keeper!

Change

These are modern days, they tell me,
A new century, they say.
Time to do thing's new, fresh and novel,
Time to abandon the old way.
As times and circumstances change,
People must adapt accordingly:
If we don't adjust to the new environment,
We'll be left on the trash heap of history.

Well, it seems like in the effort to innovate;
In the attempt to modernize,
We have to become slaves to fashion and foreign tastes,
And, alas, we have also become less wise.
It's like we have been changing so rapidly,
We ourselves just can't keep pace,
And we have thrown out traditional values,
Just to stay in this rat race!

Chorous

And so I say, bring back some of the old-old time practices,
Such as manners and industry.
We want to reclaim our cultural heritage,
To re-establish our identity.
Give us back discipline and pride of place,
Return to us our brotherhood.
Change if you want, but please, I beg,
Return peace to the neighbourhood!

Change is constant, I understand,
Nothing as permanent as this force.
But, pray tell, as we move on and up

Must we change from progress divorce?
Because it seems to me, as a young person,
That we are less blessed than we are cursed,
Since problems of all overwhelm so many people,
It is as if we are really progressing worse!

Let's take young people, these days, for example,
Especially the teenagers of our land;
If we honestly sum up their actions and attitudes,
Would the word be 'scary' or 'grand'?
I'm sure you'll agree with me that young people of this age
Change so often, they themselves don't know how or why
They simply follow the crowd; cling to every passing fad,
Clearly have no moral absolutes to stand by.

So change will come; be that as it may, some things will always stand:
Being compassionate, selfless, merciful, caring for the land.
Of course we must anticipate, prepare for and adjust to change – that's wise.
But in the rush and need to keep up with it, our values we cannot compromise!

"RUM: Ruin Unto Man."

CRIME AND VIOLENCE

Each day of our short lives
Throughout life until we're dead,
No matter who, what or where we are
Crime rears its ugly head.

Violence too, it takes its toil
And very often, it's so fatal
Together, violence with crime,
Sure threaten our survival.

These terrible two: – violence and crime –
Visit us in every fashion.
From stealing, arson, fighting, rape,
To murder and high treason

No one is safe from these two ills.
Not you, not I, not anyone.
For as long as life exists on earth
These two partners will, too, live on.

Crime causes pain, anguish and loss;
Violence contributes greatly.
And often, all that we can do
Is cry, "When, where can I find safety?"

Good news, however, I bring tonight
To all who fear these villains
Escape from crime and violence can
Be found in one place- 'tis heaven.

So let us all, that's you and me
But particularly the Law-Abiding ones of us
Get protection from violence and crime
By fully trusting in Lord Jesus

MESSAGE TO GLAMOUR GIRLS

You love to falsify your face;
You love to look unreal:
But I must be frank and tell you
That in reality, you're coarse and stale.

The lipstick that you love so much,
The fingernail and toenail polisher;
The powder, perfume, lotion, too,
Are all used to make you (look) better.

But although you try to smell so sweet,
Though you try to look so sumptuous,
You know quite well that if you take them off
You'd look and smell obnoxious!

And so you go on yet further:
You don bracelets, chains and earrings;
But you're really in a sorry state –
You just can't do without these things.

Yes, you know quite well that if you do
Try to live without these paraphernalia,
Your many (?) friends will abandon you.
Why? Your true looks will be answer!

A MESSAGE TO ALL

I am just a youth, a teenager at that,
But without hesitation I can tell everyone flat
That HIV/AIDS is a killer from hell,
Taking lives of adults, young people, even infants as well.

Why does the world allow this disease to continue
To destroy individuals, families, and societies, too?
Why can't people refrain from the actions that lead
To HIV/AIDS, and cause it to succeed?

The earth already has too many problems to face;
To allow HIV/AIDS to thrive is a massive disgrace!
There is enough information for people to know how to behave
To prevent this pandemic from being such a killer so grave.

So I ask all my teachers, relatives, friends, everyone:
Let us pledge ourselves to work in unison
To do whatever it takes to keep HIV/AIDS at bay.
Let us especially young people live decently and sensibly always.

"God has given you one face, and you make yourself another!"

Hamlet 3:1

TAKE ACTION

We hear it on the radio, read it in the news:
HIV-AIDS for its victim does choose
Persons of all races, classes and creed,
And seems to be claiming lives at an increasing speed!

Well, it's been some time now, three dozen years and more,
Since this dreaded disease began its killing galore.
The message of its danger has been spread far and wide;
Yet with this unwelcome visitor we still appear to abide!

I say it is high time, no doubt, for immediate action
To cause HIV-AIDS to cease and desist from its path of destruction!
Far too many lives-young, old, black, white, rich and poor –
Have been laid waste – are dead! – at this villain's dark door.

Let's practise with persistence, thus being unflinchingly wise,
The ABC's of prevention: Abstain, Be faithful, Condomize.
Yes, the time for real action is right now, or never!
So that HIV-AIDS does not become man's worst killer- disease ever.

HIV/ AIDS

HIV-AIDS: It's a killer real vile, Sine 1981, has taken life after life.

Millions of souls, despite age or social crust,
Have been snatched from among us, and reduced – again – to dust.

Why has this disease been allowed to survive and to flourish?
Or is it that it cannot really ever be conquered or perish?
The most brilliant minds of the planet, for years, almost ages,
Have expended so very much time and resources

To try find a cure, a remedy, a solution
To this HIV/AIDS, which kills without distinction.
Yet, year after year, in every nation and country,
This disease continues to take those we love so dearly.

The young people, particular, appear so nonchalant
To the cause and effects of this villain so rampant.
But as young chap myself, I find this attitude appalling,
Since to be infected by AIDS is so very retarding.

I issue this plea to all: young, old, and all others: Please engage in behaviours that
reduce HIV's chances.
Abstain, be faithful, be safe and be wholesome.   Let's eliminate HIV – AIDS; it's a
visitor NOT welcome.

THANKSGIVING

Thanksgiving time is here again; we pause in quietude
To say to God how much we care, to express our gratitude.

T	tells of Thanks we need must give to the Almighty One on high
H	hastens to offer Him our Hearts, so that therein He may reside
A	attests to our Appreciation, deep and real, for all His gifts
N	notes that of these blessings, sweet Nature is most rich
K	keeps kind care of Kindred, whom we cherish with delight
S	speaks of all Salvation: from sin, from fear, from night
G	gravitates toward God Himself, whose loving-kindness we don't merit
I	indicates the Intensity with which we seek His Holy Spirit
V	verifies the Vivacity of our true acts of thanks and praise
I	insists we live Inspiring lives throughout each one of our days
N	never ceases to remind us all of the importance of being Nice,
G	growing helpfully in Grace in times of peace or strife

We give thanks to God for His mercies deep, for loving us in every way,
So yes, we pause to tell Him so on this Thanksgiving Day!

NATURE

We enjoy the brilliant sunshine; we adore the flowers' scent
We are supplied with food from the sea so vast; we welcome the rain God sends
We feel thankful for the lovely trees; appreciate the grass so green
We cherish the earth that gives her fruit; we do feel the wind unseen
We love the snow, and fire, too. They really are a blessing
We need and care for animals, which help life more worth living

These are all elements of nature. Without them we cannot be.
Let's delight in and enjoy them, and thank God. He gives them free.

"All nature speaks eloquently and unanimously to the existence of an Almighty Creator God. To deny it is to be blindly dishonest."

THE GRASS

I sit

And I see the grass,

So green and shiny

Swaying in the wind, as it blows and blows
Around it,

Fresh, pretty, inviting.

It looks so grand,

So lovely,

I cannot help

But admire its splendid, immaculate beauty.

The grass,

Ever growing, never dying

Whether wind or rain, or sun or moon.

It spreads across the fields

And plains.

Oh yes! The grass so green

Reminds us all

So clearly

That GOD,

In His thoughtfulness and omniscience,

Gave this great gift to mankind
That it might

Encourage us, help us, feed us.

Sweet nature,

And the grass sublime!!!

"All flesh is Grass." Isaiah 40:6

ETHICS

Ethics are essential in our world today.
Ethics in our personal lives really should hold sway.
Ethics must guide our behavior, our attitude, our thought.
Ethics – without these, life would amount to one big nought!

As individuals, in groups, in institutions, and more,
A sense of ethics serves to assist us in reducing the allure
Of the myriad opportunities and temptations to do wrong.
Instead, it helps us, young and old, to be scrupulous and strong.

In homes, in businesses, in government, in schools,
A lack of ethics impels us, really, to act like fools.
Without this driving force, as a single unit or collectively,
People would carry on, behave and speak with utter dishonesty.

It is ethics that constrains us as we live and do let live.
It is ethics that teaches the superiority of 'give'
A code of ethics, written or not, helps to dispense with the mess
That its absence leaves in its place: pure, total selfishness.

So as a student, a young person, already I recognize
That ethics must guide us humans if we are to be wise.
Yes, in order for survival, for our efforts, for living to be worth it,
The one indispensable ingredient is a deep commitment to ethics!

HAPPINESS

Happiness is a state of mind
That makes one feel at ease;
It lets one do that which is right,
Effects actions that please.

It enables those who have it deep
Within their unique breast,
To be calm, serene and undisturbed,
Relaxed, and much at rest.

Happiness is an asset, too;
'Tis good for life and health.
The one who's happy is satisfied
With much or little wealth.

This virtue is not dependent on
The good fortunes of life;
It strives in times of good or ill,
In peacetime, or in strife.

Happiness lends longer years
To the life we live on earth;
So come on now! Let all of us
Seek happiness and mirth!

OPTIMISM

We live in times of trouble, of turmoil and of strife;
It is a time of crime and violence, of vanity and of vice.
Wars and conflicts abound aplenty; it's a never – ending rut !
Of evils and of chaos, there's an ever- growing glut.

Sometimes I sit and wonder – and I'm sure you do as well-
Whether the global situation is any better than in Hell !
The 'future' of our nations, the 'young people', they say,
Conduct themselves so vilely, it takes the light out of the day.

Yes, men and women, children, young people, all display so blatantly
Behaviours that clearly threaten our prospects for sanity.
Peace and progress seem so far off for many of us earth's populace;
No wonder so many of us seek escape in drugs and sex.

Suicide, too, some persons commit to get away from earth's despair,
Because the hope that things will improve, just seems to disappear.

But I come now to tell you that despite all the pain and gore,
OPTIMISM you must harness; OPTIMISM you must share galore.

Be an OPTIMIST, I urge you, in your thoughts and actions true!
See the light at the end of the tunnel! Let OPTIMSM become you!
Join the band of earnest persons who have found OPTIMISM's way.
Break the shackles of despondency! Be an OPTIMIST, I say!!

RESPECT

R   refers to Rectitude, reliability, right and rule

E   exhorts to Excellence; this is often stressed at school

S   of course, spells SELF-respect, without which we're bound to Lose

P   pleads with us for Patience, pride, participation- not platitudes

E   explains Example, each one of us ought to be

C   combines Compassion, Care, Concern: all three in unity

T   tells for real of tolerance, the virtue that's so high

       If we all possess these qualities, then Respect will never die!

VALUES

Values are a treasured gift
That comes from God above.
They teach, in no uncertain terms,
How to live a life of love.

They guide us in the paths of right,
They lead us to the good;
Values instruct, they edify,
They bless us, as they should.

Those of us who cherish them,
Who value them so much,
They keep us living lives sublime,
Help us to feel God's touch.

Values are real. Important, too:
Without truth, what would we be?
And patience, understanding, care,
All make life so happy!

Yes, brothers, sisters, friends and all,
Let us for values fight.
Let's practise them; let's live them out.
Let's be people of light.

DRUGS MUST GO!!

Our world's replete with troubles; evils of every sort;
And often, to find refuge, we're tempted to sniff and snort.
We feel ourselves deserted, devoid of peace and hope,
And to rid us of our despair, we resort to coke and dope.

The problem with these behaviours is that when all is done,
After we've had doses of drugs, we're back where we'd begun!
For tests – and lives – have proven without the slightest doubt,
That instead of lifting us 'on high', drugs leave us down and out.

The youth especially, we fear, pursue this course of action:
Believing – falsely, medicine shows – that drugs are good consumption.
Now today, we wail and cry at the result of all this folly,
As cigarettes, cocaine, crack, alcohol, take their toll quite deadly.

Hard work, with play, entertainment, sports, caring for mind and body,
Staying sane, healthy, alert and hale, living in decency and honesty;
These goals for all, especially young, are the true recipe for success.
No way can, or will drugs take their place; drugs cause nothing but pure mess

So pushers, users, traffickers, all, to you is made this plea:
Give up your craving for drugs so vile, abandon your greed for 'blood money'
Instead of destroying our land and youth, and causing society much pain,
Let's make our lands drugs- free and clean, make them Paradise again!!!

DRUGS ARE BAD FOR YOU

Sung to the tune of: (GO, Tell it on the Mountain.)

Our world is full of trouble; sorrow of every sort,
And often, to find solace, we're tempted to sniff and snort.

We often feel dejected, devoid of peace and hope,
SO many seek pep and power by using coke and dope

Young people in particular engage in the use of drugs,
Forgetting – or not caring – about the damage to their lungs

CHOROUS

GO, tell it from the pulpit
In the schools, and your homes too –
Go, tell form the media that drugs are bad for you!

Drugs bring false satisfaction, and transient relief,
But after their consumption, they leave only much grief

Cigarettes, ganga and cocaine, alcohol and crack as well,
Are no panacea for despair; they come direct from hell!

To all users and traffickers, I make this burning plea:
'Reject those harmful substances, and your greed for 'blood money'

Rather than cause society and our youth to bear such pain,
Let's make our land drug – free and clean, a healthy place again!'

WORK AND INDUSTRY

Work is unpleasant sometimes; it is true,
But without work, really, what would we do?
Who would perform all duties to be done?
In an A-C office, or in the blazing sun?

Yes somebody must teach, somebody must clean
Humans must entertain, be they lowly or supreme.
Nurses, electricians, shopkeepers, police,
Somebody to cook, some to sweep the street

Whatever the calling, whatever the work
Work and Industry we just cannot shirk
Without people working, life will come to a halt
And each one of us will have to bear fault

But when people work, they must be properly paid
They must be rewarded, sometimes again and again
Working conditions we must never neglect
And all workers everywhere must be treated with respect

Yes, society and the economy are dead without work,
And Industry, too. We can't allow that to irk.
But workers all over must be given their due
It's the duty of all, including me and you.

TO BE BLIND

I may be blind, unable to see, but come now and understand me clearly:
Being blind does not, and never can, signify a need or desire for pity.
For though I do not see, it's but in the physical sense; yes, it's an uncomfortable reality.
But rest assured, and know for a fact, that it is not a lethal disability.

You see, my mind is alert, my body responsive, my thoughts are formed with clarity;
And in so many very significant ways, I manage my affairs with dexterity.
I work at jobs demanding much expertise; I fulfill my duties aplenty;
I eat, sing, and play, just like you, sighted ones, and I certainly do maintain my family.

But not only that. I want you to know, that in spite of my blindness so physical,
I read and understand, make sound judgment, too, and also make decisions so critical.
I'm spiritual, too, perhaps even more so now, depending on my Creator for guidance,
Remembering now, and tomorrow, and aye, that He is the maker and giver of vision.

So the point you must grasp, the message to be learnt, is this: That blindness is no lesser
A state of affairs than sightedness, true. Being blind does not make one inferior.
This drawback, in fact, often serves to ensure that blind folks are more conscious, more careful

Than sighted individuals who, so often, you'll agree, carry themselves in a manner so forceful.

Let us now here, then, pledge and commit ourselves to this ideal so noble and lofty:
To respect all blind folks, give them their due, and treat them always with dignity.

Remember: Blindness is blind! It sees no distinction in its victims! Your neighbor today, but tomorrow, could be you. Let's co-exist with each other with compassion.

Headmaster: "Son, what is your name?"
Student: "Walter"
Headmaster: Don't you know you must say 'sir' when talking to me? Now, what is your name?"
Student: "Sir Walter!"

OUR CULTURE

People everywhere, both present and past
Cherish and practise some habits that endure and last.
From generation to generation, year in and out,
These habits and customs we call 'our culture', no doubt

Our music, our dress, our architecture, our food-
These unique expressions do make us feel good.
Our dance, our dialect, our tastes, our values
Are all special features which our culture imbues

Our people may come, and go our people may,
But our culture, well, that is sure here to stay.
It is what defines us, makes us stands out as special.
We must define our culture; it's a duty most crucial

Culture comes in forms that are tangible, sure:
Architecture, Industries, Literature, food and more.
It is also intangible, to behold, not to be held –
Our thoughts, patterns, speech forms, lore, heritage.

Our culture defines us; it makes us stand out.
It denotes us as a people, unique in the crowd.
No nation or society is ever complete, you see,
Without a clear set of features: its cultural identity

Let's cherish, safeguard and preserve our culture!

ARTICLE

THE CASE FOR INTRODUCING 'PARENTING' EDUCATION IN SCHOOLS

Many persons are convinced – and statistics seem to buttress their belief – that the increasing and disconcerting palpable rise in incidences of robbery, burglary, wounding, shooting, killing and general violence is being perpetrated largely by young people, particularly males.

Sociologists have long established that it is violent crime, which by definition and practice always claims a victim, that citizens fear most, relative to other types of criminal acts.

This, of course, is quite understandable, as self-preservation is the first order of business, so to speak, first on the list of priorities for almost all of mankind. And violent crime, with its inherent threat to life and limb, directly opposes that superlative and supreme principle.

Violent crime often draws or threatens to draw blood, the essence of life. And the fact that each such act directly or indirectly, in one way or another, affects multiple individuals and families (given the realities of historically and culturally close kinship ties. No man is an island, after all.), means that in a very real sense, violent crime affects us all.

But it is not only violent crime that one must fear. In fact, violent crime is neither a cause nor an end in and of itself. Social Scientists unanimously agree that crime is a complex phenomenon whose causes and solutions are as manifold and intractable as any social problem, and more so than most.

Certainly, collective society must be altogether concerned about young people's general sociopathic behaviours, as manifested so readily, easily, pervasively and ubiquitously in repeated acts of disrespect (for self and others , including their person, reputation and property), aggression, impatience, indecency, foul language, immodest dress, inability to reason, lack of compassion, indolence, insolence, disregard for authority, and embrace of mediocrity, among other negatives.

However, it is crime, violent crime, that obviously draws the most reaction and generates the most fear.

(Of course, I need not labour the FACT that very many, no doubt MOST of our young people, our young men, are NOT engaged in criminal activity!)

But since very much, in fact most of the serious 'blue-collar' crimes are apparently committed by 'misguided youths', many citizens / residents are quick to point the accusing finger at two major institutions in society, the Home and the School, as the breeding ground for these malevolents, and lay the blame for this malaise squarely at their feet. (The Church, too, is often accused of failing in its duty to help restrain youngsters from evil-doing.)

And perhaps they are right. The fact of the matter is that these crime-committers (persons generally ages 18 – 30) are, far more likely than not, simply outputting what they took in during their formative years (from birth to adolescence), when, of course, almost all of their daylight/ waking hours are spent at home and / or at school.

This means that parents and teachers failed miserably in their duty and responsibility to properly train, discipline, instruct and guide their children and students in a way that steers them away from being perpetrators and / or victims of crime in general, violent crime more so.

Further, it must be emphasized that notwithstanding the fact that most of the active daylight hours are sent at school for 36 or so weeks of the calendar year, it is a myth is subscribed to by many that teachers and/or peers exert more influence on young people, particularly adolescents, than do their parents.

The truth is that field and action research, both in and beyond the region, has revealed, unambiguously, that it is the PARENT who still occupies that position, who exercises more/ most influence on students' behaviour, conduct and attitude.

If, then, we are to accept that young people acquire a propensity for violence during their development stages, then it stands to reason that parents carry the major portion of responsibly for their children, our young people's actions.

And this is one major reason why the need, the call for Parenting education in schools is clarion, clear, and compelling.

Parents are the first teachers that children know and meet, anyway. But parents, like others, cannot teach what they do not know. They cannot lead to where they do not go. And, by and large, they do NOT know how to properly and correctly parent a child. (Of course, some are definitely desirous of being good parents.)

The role of education as an institution is paramount in this scenario. My posit is that it is the formal school system and setting wherein the dynamics and details of parenting must be introduced, exposed, imparted.

Lamentably, the current generation of parents 'at fault' is difficult to reach in terms of effectuating the types of changes in parenting styles envisaged and desired. But for the sake of the future of society, to save upcoming generations, to see and enjoy a marked reduction in the myriad acts of wanton violence, cruelty, animosity, delinquency and other dehumanizing, inhuman acts being visited by man upon man, we ought to fitfully introduce Parenting as a discrete, core-curricula subject in our nation's schools with immediacy.

Another major reason for such an innovation resides in the fact that whereas students, both males and females, upon exiting the formal school environment, will inevitably pursue a plethoric, eclectic multitude and variety of jobs/occupations/careers, it is simply inarguable that, realistically, upward of 90% of them will become PARENTS, some sooner than others, many several times over.

Clearly, something is patently amiss with a system that expands much time, energy, expertise, money and effort in preparing our students/young people for the world of adulthood which all (barring death) will attain, and for the world of work, which many will enter, but we do nothing or hardly anything deliberate, systematic, strategic or syngenetic to ready and prepare them for the role of parenthood, which most will assume.

Room can and must be found to accommodate Parenting in the curriculum. In any event, there already exists a crying need to revisit and reform the curriculum content to eliminate the duplication, redundancies and irrelevancies that suffocate it, and have it more meaningfully reflect and represent a set of learning experiences germane to the times.

Finally, I propose that Parenting education begin at Grade 3, and run the gamut until 5th Form, and that it includes in its instructional content the following emphases, inter alia: the social, spiritual, moral, physical, emotional and educational needs of children, and roles of parents in this respect; challenges and demands of single parenting; child development; kinship; protection and support of children; love vs. infatuation; virtues of chastity, abstinence and fidelity; competition; relationships; the manifold responsibilities of mothers and fathers; training and discipline of children; dangers of early sex and pregnancy; life chances; benefits of two-parent families; sanctity of marriage; costs of child rearing; role modelling; health issues; legal implications; culture, customs, norms, mores and values; and other relevant topics.

The crucial questions of WHO imparts this instruction, and the training requisite for them, are to be decided upon subsequent to the necessary sober, intense discussions and conversations attendant with this process.

But the potential for Parenting in schools to have constructive, positive effects on the outlook, behavior, thinking and attitude of students, which will translate into better-behaved, more anti-sociopathic, less violent children and, by extension, a safer, more secure harmonious society, is immense and untapped. It begs for the dialogue to begin.

So let the discourse re Parenting in schools start in earnest. Now

Published by:

www.purposefulauthors.com

Affiliated with:

Author's Contact:

TEL: 1-869-669-0984

Email: sylvesterblake137@yahoo.com

www.ingramcontent.com/pod-product-compliance
Lightning Source LLC
LaVergne TN
LVHW051846080426
835512LV00018B/3106